How to Un-F*ck Your Vibration

The Twin Flame Edition

By: Kris Embrey

Contents

Thank You 1
Foreword 2
What is a Twin Soul or Twin Flame? 6
The Twin Flames: The Secret Society 7
I'm Seeing Shit 12
Keeping People Out the Connection 18
My Twin, My Problem 20
The Signs are Confusing 22
Numerology 1-9 25
Why am I on a Twin Soul Journey? 27
Twin Flames the Unconditional Love Story 29
Surrender: Choosing the Road Upward 32
Un-F Your Vibration 33
Universal Laws 37
Twin Catalyst vs. True Twin Love 42
The Dark Side of the Twin Flame Connection 44
About the Author 47

Thank You

This book is dedicated to all of the Twin Flames - May the journey with your counterpart be loving, and all that you've ever had hoped for.

To All Twin Flame Guides, the work you do is so important, and is appreciated a million times over. Thank you for being there for us.

For my Twin, under the strangest of circumstances we met. When I look back there's *nobody* I'd rather taken the journey with. You're loved unconditionally now and always.

Contents in this book are intended to help those navigate the Twin Flame journey. If you feel that you need to seek professional help due to your Twin Flame connection, it is advised for you to do what is best for you. I'm not a licensed therapist, just someone who has experienced a Twin Flame connection. I do not identify myself as a Twin Flame guide. My intention is to share through writing, and help those look at things from a Universal point-of-view, while finding their own inner peace, and self-love through periods of separation with their beloved Twin counterparts. Always know that you are loved now and always.

This book is copyrighted through WGA
Registration Number: 1899622
Quotes used is the book are credited to their original owner.
Twin Flames information was provided through personal experience.

Foreword

I met my Twin Flame the same day my first book was released, Tell Me You Want Me; a fictional romance novel that manifested my Twin counterpart cover to cover literally in April of 2016. I started out like most TF on this journey; meeting a really nice guy, we connected, after three dates poof…

After four months of no physical contact, and polite text messages back and forth, I started experiencing an incredible amount of synchronicities on a daily basis that seem to connect back to him, in a very odd way. The message for me was hidden in a song lyric, that connected a meaning, followed by a confirmation of finding a dime afterwards, linking the two together.

The sign of song/dime combo continued several months to the point it was making me a little nuts.

Four-months had gone by with no physical contact, and towards the last month we stopped communicating all together. When this happened, a bombardment of signs followed that centered around him, with no logical explanation for me to understand.

Some of those signs consisted of number patterns, songs, and dimes that I found appearing to be strategically placed around my car for me, to take notice. Since I hadn't tried to sort out the meaning of these signs prior, the Universe decided one afternoon in July 2016, that I would be witness to a quantum physics phenomena that involved my car radio, flipping stations to the same song over and over, and a religious medallion (not belonging to me) that had the words Trust in Jesus, that came bolting down from the roof of my car and landing on my leg as I was driving. It was on that day I decided to wake-up/look to find an answer for what I'd experienced, because it wasn't normal.

A month later, after failed attempts getting answers from tarot readers, and religious theologians on what I had been experiencing with signs, my Twin counterpart re-entered my path. The day my Twin reached out; those earlier signs I'd been seeing for months, had set me up for this re-connection to take place. I was tested by my counterpart when he sent me a text message after four-months of no physical contact *"what time do you get off work?"* I clearly saw those signs flashing back to me as I waited to reply back; *"I'm out of town."*

My history with men was not the best, and it was something I was in the process during those months, healing in myself. My self-worth had always been an issue for me. I'm an attractive person, but my core issue; I'm the nice girl, and the nice girl gets shit on, guys don't want nice. Their mothers, and grandmothers are nice. Men want to chase, hunt, and kill the tiger bitch. I'm still working on my nice girl issue, but became wiser to my core issue of being to accommodating. And it was because of those signs.

It's important to remember that you may see your relationship to your Twin as the Divine relationship, but it does not mean that common sense and dating rules still do not apply, they do, especially if you have an unawakened Twin counterpart you're dealing with. Sleeping with your Twin before you really get to know them will not guarantee union, in fact it could really screw you up and set the relationship back.

Before going any further in this book, I want to advise; not everything in this book will resonate with you, and that is OK. Unfortunately, the higher powers did not leave behind a Twin Flames guidebook, or roadmap for this type of relationship. The compass inside of you should always serve as your inner-knowing on what information is right for you at any given time, when it resonates, its right, when it doesn't, it's not for you.

We're all are in various stages of the journey. It depends on where you're at spirituality, when new information gets downloaded and will click for you. This information is received based on your soul growth. As you learn about the Twin Flame journey, you'll be helping others who magically come onto your path. It's a very natural process.

Each sovereign journey will be unique, but the principal for all is the same, you have met *the one* and you're evolving spiritually because of the experience. You've been awakened.

I realize some of you are still caught on the Twin Flame relationship aspect of the journey, and you'll need patience grasshopper, learn it now if it's not a trait you currently have, you'll need to master it.

The Twin Flame journey is the test of one's patience, a soul evolution and awaking all happening simultaneously. Meeting a Twin Flame isn't just about meeting *the one*, It's a wake-up call to get you onto your life mission.

Twin Flames have one commonality that connects us all; we're here to spirituality grow from the experience. At times on this journey you probably felt like it's The Hunger Games version of getting into union. Another commonality amongst the TF group, seems to be that we've signed-up to take on this mission of unconditional love. That's nice and all, but self-love is also very important.

Everyone on the Twin Flame path is at a different level spirituality. Each individual will have experiences that will differ based on each individual's own level of karma they need to work on. Let me repeat that, We're working out karma, personal, and ancestral DNA karma before birth. Some of you may have been through some pretty traumatic experiences, depending on the level of karma being worked through and with your counterpart.

Some of you will be in happy relationships right out of the gate with their Divine counterparts, and some won't. Each Twin Flame relationship is unique to each couple. There're are no guarantees of "Twindom," no time restrictions can be imposed to meet a "union" deadline, no planetary shifts can predict when you'll be in a relationship with your Twin counterpart, and seeing the number 1111 is not a requirement for entering into a relationship with your Twin Flame. The goal for all is the same; the road to learning, self-love, then unconditional love will follow.

You may be saying, "I just want to know how to spear the fish before the next planetary shift, forget that light-worker stuff, I want to be with my person." Believe me I want that for you as well, but if you're not in communication with your Twin right now, that focus you've placed on your Twin, needs to be put back on YOU not the relationship aspect to this journey. That key piece of information will save you months of grief. Take it from someone who spent over a year and a ton of money on people that knew nothing more than I did about what I was going through in the Twin Flame experience. Work on you, and the meaning to those signs always reveal themselves at the right moment, and in the right time when you are to know.

Getting into a relationship with you're Twin comes down to two very basic principals; the work you are willing to invest in yourself, and what your soul contract had written for you to experience before you were born. That's it. This information is here to help you navigate in peace, not talk you down from the tree of Twindom. Love to all of the Twin's.

What is a Twin Soul or Twin Flame?

Twin Flame and Twin Souls are the same. The title is whatever you choose to call yourself, but not to be confused with soul-mates. The latter is based more in the love and lust department. The term Twin Flame does get over-used at times, and perhaps for various reasons. I actually refer to this relationship model as a Divine Soul Connection. But labels are just that, labels. It is whatever you wish to identify yourself as. You choose what you like. For this book I will use the terms TF, Twin Flame, Twin, or Divine Counterpart.

Twin relationships hold some deeper meaning than that of the typical soul-mate relationships. Likely, when you met your Twin, it was under an unusual circumstance. The relationship with our Twin counterpart has more to do with developing creativity, learning, growing, and healing for the soul's journey. It's not *just* about a relationship with your Twin counterpart. Twin connections help us to become better versions of ourselves.

If you've encountered a Twin that is physically abusive towards you, then I implore you to seek professional council, and a spiritual healer to help safely transition away from this person by doing energy work and cord cutting. However, for this book, I'll be focusing on non-abusive connections, as I'm not a licensed therapist and can only speak to what I've experienced.

The Twin Flames: The Secret Society

Like so many that will go through this amazing experience of finding our perfect match, it seems from the beginning of meeting to be Divine design, and in all cases it was. The stories seem to be the same; you've met the person of your dreams, you found out that you have so many things in common, and this wonderful person really gets you like nobody else. You're able to finish each other's thoughts, almost like you share the same brain. But it was when you paused for a moment in time, looked into their eyes, and found home with this person, like you knew them from a previous life. They just seem familiar to you, and you just want to see *that look* in their eyes again.

By now you are three or four dates in, and thinking to yourself, *"This is really too good to be true."* Several weeks have gone by, no phone calls, no text messages, and you wait. It's getting close to the weekend, and you decide to go ahead and send that text message. You get a fast reply, *"Sorry out of town,"* your heart sinks. You can't stop thinking about them, but your counterpart seems distant and really busy. A few weeks go by, and just when you give-up on ever seeing them again, strange signs started pouring on you like rain.

A few more weeks go by, and it seems obvious this person disappeared for no apparent reason, but wait... there was a reason...When you were thinking; *this is too good to be true*, your counterpart perhaps experienced that also, only they heard it in their head this way, *"stranger danger, did they put some kind of hex on me?"* and away they went. The energy transmitted between the two of you was so intense when you looked into his/her eyes. What each of you saw was the gateway into your very own souls.

This is the beginning stages of the term called Twin Flame Runner. Not everyone will have to go through it, and bless those who don't, but the majority of TF's do. Those who've experienced running/ghosting by their Twin counterpart likely spent countless hours wondering what *you* did wrong. By now you've become obsessed with decoding the meaning of Angel numbers, and you hold an honorary doctorate degree in numerology, and an honorary master's in the number 1111. Your accountant has mentioned at least once, *"You can't write psychics off anymore as therapy*." Congratulations: you've officially met your Twin Flame. The feeling of *the one* when you looked into their eyes.

You had no prior knowledge of what a Twin Flame was, and perhaps thought this person was probably your soul-mate when you started seeing odd signs, and wondered; is this fate? It must be, Wow! This is just like a movie, awesome!

Hold-up …fast forward. It is three-months later, and that movie seems to be more like the Matrix. Your heart hurts, you think about him/her and you can't figure out why. Welcome to the Secret Society of Twin Flames. You've been initiated into Twin Flamedom without your ever knowing it. You're a hot mess, crying and carrying on about someone you hardly know, *but your heart knows*. And this is where I say: STOP pining. Yes they are your Twin, but they ghosted you, how are you going to deal with it? I have some helpful tools we will uncover later in this book.

The intense vibe is what sent them running and it's keeping you from the connection with your Twin counterpart. There is a runner chaser phase only if you allow it to be a phase,. If they run and you chase, then it's a phase.

You have awoken your Twin's issues and that's why they went running. Depending on their personality, they will run back. The reason? Some have narcissism issues in their DNA bloodline and will likely be working through those issues.

Emotions play a big part on this journey, and whether those emotions are positive, or negative, they're emotions felt at the soul level. These feelings with your counterpart are amplified and over-exaggerated compared to the so-called *normal* relationship. When things are good with your Twin, it feels great, but it's when things are not going so well with your Twin that those feelings can be amplified. The reason? There's more emotional energetic intensity between Twin Flames. Those interactions you have with your Twin are happening on a soul level, and it can become an emotional roller coaster ride for you both when you are absorbing each other's emotions in the same physical space.

Your Twin counterpart may not be as in touch with *their* feelings, but in your presence, they feel that something is weird, and they don't know why.

Keeping your *emotions* in check in the presence of your Twin early into the beginning stages of meeting your counterpart (especially if they are not as open or as spirituality advanced as you) is best advised. As your relationship with your Twin grows, then those feelings should be talked about and explored, and you'll know when that time is right. There is no set length of time. You'll just know when it *feels right* for you to have that conversation with your Counterpart. Some people are more open than others, but from personal experience, the runner is not typically as open to discussing any "feelings or emotions" a few months into knowing them. You have to look at your own personal situation and relationship dynamic between each other, to see what is right for you. Everyone is different. Take into consideration that if your Twin is coming out of a divorce type situation, or longer relationship perhaps they are not looking to have "the feelings talk" at this point in time; they may need to heal from the situation they are learning from. However with that said, some Twins are "needy" and need to be comforted by others. You have to decide for yourself; go inward and ask for guidance from Source. We'll all have our own unique situation when it comes to discussing feelings with our Divine Counterparts; if you do decide to open up to them with your feelings be honest with what is in your heart.

I will share with you that I told my Twin that I was in love with him after knowing him almost a year. After I shared my feelings he didn't run, but he also did not not reciprocate the word "love" until a few months later, and we are not in a "relationship" but, it felt really good after I told him what was in my heart. Again, you have to make your own choice of what is right for **you**. I share this example to help you, not give advice on what you should do. Always go with what is in your heart. That is key!

If we shift for a moment and look at Twin Flame emotions as spiritual development from a perspective of learning in school it may be helpful.

When you entered into first grade you learned the very basic fundamentals of spelling. When you got to high school you learned more, and into college, more learning was applied. Looking at emotions from the perspective of the spiritual development of one's soul, and from a perspective of learning, this will help you navigate the pining away, and focus on your becoming more elevated spirituality to handle these high emotions and be ready for your Twin Flame union. I've put together some helpful emotional release practices in the chapter *how to un-f your vibration*, to help you along the way.

Learning emotional detachment in this running phase is the best advice I can give. Detachment simply means to have no expectations on the outcome with your Twin counterpart, no matter how many tarot readers say "this is your Twin, this is the one" that messaging creates attachment. Having detachment of your emotions and the outcome of the union will actually help move you more into the union if it is designed to happen for you in that way.

Energetically at the running/ghosting phase, is the start of a cleansing process where you'll be working through some heavy duty layers of garbage that stem from childhood, or some form of past trauma, either in this lifetime or previous lifetimes. Translation: you both have issues/baggage that need clearing out, and when you're in the presence of your Twin, those core issues are amplified to a level ten. This is the journey: to look inward and fix yourselves, not each other, so you can move upward in your lives, and create space for the union or reunion to occur.

The intensity of emotions starts the separation/ghosting phase, and it seems almost inevitable, due to the circumstances of meeting our Twin in the first place. Unless both Twins are spiritually developed, you'll likely go through some period of separation, and nobody can predict for how long it can last. It all depends on you doing the work you need to do on you, but still there are no guarantees due to the free-will choices that we are all governed by.

The union with your Twin is dependent on *you* fixing *you*. The faster you can work on yourself and those core issues, the faster they can come running back.

The running-chasing phase as it's called, is when you start transmuting/purging old wounds and ancestral garbage. You're being called by higher powers to start dealing with those shadows of the dark self. When you looked into the eyes of your Twin counterpart, things that you both needed to work on came to the surface as you locked eyes for the first time.

You and your Twin counterpart each hold an invisible mirror, reflecting what needs to be healed within yourselves. This is the secret society known as Twin Flames; it's a healing journey of the souls. You both signed up for this journey. It was written in your soul contract before you were born. The meeting of your Twin counterpart was destined or fated to happen.

I'm Seeing Shit

When you met your Twin, you may have experienced some confusing signs before you ever met them, and may even had a dream about them.

When you met, time seemed to fly by, and you could have found yourself in some synchronic alignment to your Twin as far as commonalities. You had very similar backgrounds, but yet opposite, and similar all at the same time.

Signs are a big part of the Twin Flame experience. I personally hated it when someone said to me, *"the signs are not for the reasons you think, it's a warning."* Screw that. I also had a distain for, *"ignore the signs, you need to love yourself."* It's really hard to ignore what's in front of your face, but know you're not going crazy. Signs are as real as you want to experience them. Pay attention to what you were thinking about at the time you saw the sign. The answer you seek may be hidden there.

- **When I met my Twin we had all of these signs, what do they mean?** Ah, the synchronicities, those meaningful coincidences that have us going into detective mode for hours on end to figure out their meaning. The signs that move together in time and space and happen when a thought occurs in the mind and then mirrors back to us by an external event, or perhaps the signs took you by complete surprise and knocked the wind out of you. You've heard songs on the radio, and even seen their name on buildings and street signs. Congrats, you've entered the gateway to Twin Flamedom when you encountered the number 1111 prior, during, and after you met the other half of your soul. The signs are set-up as billboards on your path and is the soul's way of recognizing that the connection you've made will be the most important connection of your life. It's the soul's way of reminding you to stay on your path. The Twin meeting is the journey back to Source, it's the journey home. If you had a thought while seeing a sign, recall what you were thinking about, and it can shed some light on the answer to the question. The Universe used to play with me, giving me a song lyric followed by a dime. You have to apply the sign to fit your situation, once you learn the way Source communicates with you. It will likely use that same method over and over. Only you can decipher the sign and your first gut reaction is usually the correct one to the answer.

- **I'm still seeing signs during separation.** That's great, signs can be the Universe's way of saying "you're on the right track" and only you can decide for yourself what it means to you. Always go with your first gut reaction.
- **Massive power outages.** This sign seems to defy logic, but it's common. It has been said that when someone is vibrating on a high emotional level it can effect electricity. When Twins are vibrating high, they can manipulate lights and energy around them when together.
- **Everyone says love myself, what does that mean really?** This is one concept that people have the most problem with, and I get it. The Twin Flame journey is about love of self and unconditional love. It took me a year on my Twin journey for this message to connect to my brain. I thought I had to do things for my Twin to get his attention, and to show respect for our connection. WRONG. By not focusing on myself, I was pushing my Twin further from me. It takes time for the self-love thing to click and make sense, but when it does, everything unlocks inside and is waiting for you. Loving yourself means many things to many people, but if you're experiencing separation/ghosting, or not, use this precious time to do something *you* have always wanted to do: travel, start that new job, learn a new trade, call a friend, do something that *you* enjoy. When you turn that love inwards to making yourself happy you're raising your vibration, and also that love of self gets reflected back to your Twin, because they are energetically part of you. Practice self-love and watch what unfolds. Self-love is not just self-empowering, but giving love to your Twin unconditionally in the process.
- **Why do I see signs and my Twin doesn't?** There is a circular answer to this. Some Twin Flames have childhood issues that need healing, and we all have ancestral crap we

need to work on that is embedded in our DNA. The connection you share with your Twin is a past you shared in other timelines and dimensions. You both more than likely experienced some form of childhood trauma, be it neglect, abuse, dismissive parenting, or childhood bullying. You, being the more spiritually awakened Twin, experience the sign communication and will be the one who will clear-out the garbage for you both, while your counterpart does not see any signs because they are not yet awake. The clearing that you do on you, your Twin benefits from. This would have been agreed upon and written into your soul contract before birth.

- **What if I manifested my Twin?** Manifestations at the most basic level are thoughts, be them positive or negative; like attracts like. Focus on something long enough, and it shall come to pass. If you had thoughts about meeting *the one* most of your adult life, it's the soul's way of recognizing your Twin. It's a universal law, The Law of Attraction.
- **What about Freewill of the souls?** I have a core belief that when you met your Twin, it was fated. Freewill on both sides was revoked and the meeting was Divinely orchestrated. However, there is the Universal law of freewill. Most events in your life are astrologically and karma predestined, you have freewill to transform the impact of any event in your life, including Twin Flame relationships. You and your Twin possess at anytime a freewill choice to avoid the relationship entirely. This freewill does result from how you have lived your life up to the situations you have set for yourself to experience. If you are positive, loving, compassionate, and demonstrate by your actions that you have come to this planet to learn lessons, you'll minimize unpleasant experiences. Everyone has freewill in how they choose to respond to any situation. There is no law that says, *my twin must be with me happily and forever after.* Only time will tell that.
- **When I met my Twin, they were involved in another relationship**. This is a very common issue among the Twin Flame community. When you meet your mirrored soul, it's

usually at the most challenging time in your life for one, or both Twins. Not in all cases, but the majority seems to prevail. Typically, one of the Twins will be unavailable in some way, whether that means being emotionally unavailable or being involved in another relationship and must finish their learning before they can fully commit to you or anyone.

- **Are all Twin relations romantic?** Not all Twin relationships are romantic. Most of them can be and usually are at some point in the relationship, but it depends on both people and the choices they make to move the relationship forward. Remember, The Law of Freewill prevails for all beings. Your Twin will at some point be awoken because of you through the work you do on yourself. The connection you made with your Twin is beneficial for you both, and you are forever connected by an unseen invisible cord.
- **My Twin ran away, now what?** I don't believe in the concept of runner-chaser; however, it comes up a lot so I'll explain. The running Twin usually leaves due to the magnetic energy after meeting. This energy is so intense in the beginning that it creates confusion, stopping any of the romantic feelings. You're both being guided by Source during this separation, to look inside yourselves and fix what you need to within yourselves.
- **Will he/she come back?** If you're asking this question you need to change the focus on how you are asking it. Your Twin has never "left you" as they are energetically connected to you always. Change the perception of loss to reinventing themselves to a new 10.0 version, raising you and your Twin's vibration. But to answer the question from my own experience, yes they will contact you again, but there're no time tables, and no rules as to the *when* part. Take this time and thank Source for the blessing. The separation happened not because of anything *you did;* it's so you both can focus on yourselves to be better humans. Do the inner work on yourself and it will no doubt speed up the process for your Twin to reach out and re-connect with you. They will feel the change within you.

- **Are the signs coincidence or synchronicity?** There are no coincidences in in life. Coincidences are nothing more than synchronic events; only the person who sees the sign will be the one who has the experience. It would not be a coincidence if your Twin has the same type of experience with a sign as you. It's how each of you interpret the sign as to it's meaning. If having some difficulties in seeing a clear answer to a sign, you can purchase a deck of oracle cards, choose a deck that calls to you. Shuffle the cards, lay them out, ask the question, and choose a card. It could shed some light to the question you have.
- **Should I tell my Twin they are my Twin Flame?** Never. Your Twin counterpart needs to figure out their own spiritual journey. Remember, you both are working on your own stuff in different ways. It's counterproductive to send your Twin counterpart TF e-mail links, or have conversations about TF topics, unless they come to you first. Bringing up topics of TF will likely anger them if they are not yet spiritually awake. Your Twin counterpart has their own learning to be completed at their own sovereign pace.
- **What sign do I need to see before we come back together?** There is no definite sign. You may experience increased signs, or have an increased sense of awareness of your counterpart, but I advise not to put a ton of emphasis on it. Divine timing dictates union with your Twin, always.
- **What is a False Twin Flame?** A false Twin is a karmic partner with signs, but the signs have no correlation to the person directly unless you are looking at a photo, and the person calls you, or something similar to that. If you find yourself repeating the same arguments with a partner over and over again, you might be in a karmic relationship. These repeated patterns mean that you have not learned from the karmic lesson that is being shown to you. The opportunity for personal growth is to break the pattern and learn what caused you to go back and repeat the lesson over.
- **Divine timing, what is it?** That means if you are to be with your Twin, it will happen in Divine timing. You have zero

control on the pace of the union. The union will happen if it's meant to happen.

Keeping People Out the Connection

As you embark on your Twin Flame mission, aligning yourself with a spiritual team is as important as the journey itself. It is imparted on you to keep all conversations about your Twin Flame limited to people that have spiritual knowledge that you can trust. If you don't have a spiritual friend, or know of another Twin Flame couple, you can go to You Tube and type Twin Flame, search for guides who have messaging you like and follow them. We have some really great teachers out there. Know that you're never without resources.

Taking into consideration that this is not a normal relationship, your family and friends will have a difficult time understanding *your obsession*, unless they've gone through the Twin Flame experience for themselves. You can expect they'll have challenges/think you are crazy, as to understand what you are talking about when it comes to signs. Pulling people in that have not experienced this type of relationship model for advice, you'll likely invite more confusion onto yourself. Expecting people to understand a spiritual contracted soul connection, is like speaking English to someone who only speaks Greek. They won't understand everything, only bits and pieces, not to mention they won't believe you, and it can create more confusion and monkey mind in your brain space.

If you do choose to do this, don't be surprised when your friends and family suggest seeing a therapist or the family priest. I'm not here to knock any therapy, and if you do choose to seek professional help, find someone who has compassion for the Twin Flame community. I've spent thousands of dollars talking to everyone from theologians, to tarot readers. Finding someone you can trust that has knowledge of Twin Flame connections is advised.

Understanding the importance of staying silent about the synchronicity and signs you're experiencing, including talking about them early on with your Twin trust me, the deer in the headlight look is priceless. If you don't want them running for the hills, lay low on synchronicity talk.

The friends that are in your life may have had in the past, some control or influence over your life. You know the friends, who always need to be right, or the friends that look at you as if you have lost your mind when you say, *"Twin Flame."* They say things like, "*why are you putting all of your eggs in his basket?*" or my favorite, "*go out with someone else. Screw that guy.*" If a friend tries to manipulate the connection you have with your Twin, instant karma is usually served for the interference. If this happens to a friend, do not point it out as karma. It is best advised to stay quiet on karmic issues and let it play out and stay out. I've seen this happen in my own Twin experience. Confronting karmic lessons to others can set you back, and you loose a feather or two in the karmic realm, so don't invite the drama. Twin connections are a party of two, not three or more.

Compassion is the fine art of learning to tune-out friend chatter. Use caution when engaging in talk about your dating life. Engaging in negative speak about your Twin is really ill advised, as it is like speaking bad about yourself and why would you do that? You wouldn't. Keeping people in limited information about your Twin connection until it develops into some sort of dating phase, I've found to be very useful information.

Jealous friends can manipulate your Twin Flame relationship and set you way back. If you believe that your Twin is *the one* then you should always go with that truth, surrender, and trust in Source. Believe and trust what is in your heart over what anyone tells you about your Twin. They don't know, and it's OK.

My Twin, My Problem

You, more than likely, are the more spirituality advanced Twin, your Twin is out with friends possibly doing old paradigm behaviors of drinking, drugs, and the karmic hook-up now and then, and you're at home pining away for them.

Flippant behavior from our un-awoken Twin counterpart on this journey seems to be a common issue, but that does not mean your Twin gets to wipe their feet on you like a doormat. Forget that and stand your ground. Don't worry about pissing-off your Twin by standing up for yourself; in fact, you should as you deserve to be respected. Hell, you're the one doing all of the energy-clearing work, and respect is the bare minimum they can do for you; though I would stay hushed about the energy-clearing part with your counterpart, *they won't get it.*

You asked for this journey either in the 3-D paradigm or before you incarnated to this planet, and because you asked, you're now being awoken to the spiritual call of enlightenment. It's going to be a ride; one you'll never forget.

The one thing you have that organic relationships don't have is that built-in gravitational pull on your chakra systems. They can run, but they can't disconnect the cord.

Some of you won't have to experience bad behavior from your counterpart and bless you, for you are the lucky ones. There will likely be some challenges along the way that you may encounter, friends who want to talk you out of your Twin relationship without consciously knowing why, but what's really happening is on a subconscious level. They don't want you to have a spiritual partner; they want the old you, the one who will never change. After meeting your Twin, that old you is going to slowly evolve and be re-born into a more beautiful, enlightened, and prosperous soul.

The relationship with your Twin is not to be confused with a soul-mate type of relationship which does not typically last forever. What you're experiencing with the Twin connection was pre-designed by Source, it was fated. But not for the reason everyone thinks. There will be some disagreements about that statement, but I believe it to be very true. Really want to test the waters on this? Tell your Twin counterpart that you were fated to meet and see what happens. More than likely they will be angered. It means they didn't have a freewill choice in the matter. The fated part has nothing to do with love, it was fated because you have garbage to work on separately and together.

Whatever you decide for yourself as truth in fate will always be the right answer. That's the best part about this journey; you know what you know, and all of us will have different experiences. We all know different things from our experiences on this journey.

Your Twin relationship can have extreme highs and lows, dark nights of the soul, anxiety, and yes, separation of friends you may have had for years. Your life is getting ready to change in such a way you can't even imagine, but it's all for the betterment of you. Don't want to spend sad nights alone? Trust me, I did a full year of the pity party of one, and it wasn't worth the year of tears spent. Just because you met *the one*, don't stop living your life. Get out there and enjoy it, that is what you are suppose to be doing. This is the lesson, and this is true for every Twin Flame.

Each Twin journey will be unique and it depends on what each person has aligned themselves to learn on their own sovereign journey. This really comes down to you and what was pre-decided before you incarnated; fate that turns into love ever after, friendship of two people, or a deep soul experience. Each journey will be unique unto itself. There is an assumption that if you do the inner work that is needed to move a relationship further into union, then it is fated to be the greatest love story you could have ever written for yourself.

The Signs are Confusing

Oh these damn Twin Flame signs. If I had a dollar for every sign I'd be a millionaire. The signs are heart communication that you're here to serve your life purpose/calling, and to stay the course for your soul journey. You really need to tap into those childhood dreams you once had and explore them. I'm being very serious about this. Look at those dreams and see how you can apply them today. No matter how crazy or out of touch *you think* those dreams may be, they are not.

When seeing signs, show gratitude for them and focus inward on love for yourself. Don't waste your life away looking for signs from the Universe to give you confirmation if your Twin is *the one.* You'll be looking for signs that you actually manifested, bringing more confusion onto yourself and taking you off your path for awhile.

If you are seeing a massive amount of signs, congratulations, you possess the power to manifest, but let me impart this piece of wisdom. It's a story about the Master and the Mature. They can both do the same job, the difference is a Master takes years to develop certain talents, never getting destroyed by their job. The Master never is in need to ask for signs. A Mature will cut corners, does not want to work hard on themselves, then sits back and waits for something to happen, but the Mature gets knocked around with more lessons to learn and the journey ends up taking longer. While the Master keeps his emotions in balance and stays on his path.

Here are some of the common and not so common Twin Flame signs. See what resonates with you.

- **The number 1111:** Typically viewed as the gateway or manifestation number in the beginning of one's Twin Flame journey. Don't waste time in sorting out Angel numbers, because they are based in numerology, and numerology only goes from 1-9. Each number carries it's own meaning and vibration. So why the 1111? From a spiritual perspective, it's the number of creation, the primal force from which all other numbers move forth. When you understand the place and function of this most primal of all numbers, you'll know all there is to know and enlightenment is yours. This statement, of course, does not apply to an understanding of the number 1 from a Numerologist's perspective alone, but perhaps a good place to start. It is elevated in spiritual symbolism. Therefore, the number 1111 is magnified to get your attention. You may have other numbers, but 1111 is the most common. The other commonality is 444. Four is the number of fate, so it can be remembered as the number of many things that happen over which you have no control; magnified by the power of 3 it's a powerful number.

- **Electrical outages**; With having experienced my own electrical phenomena, I can attempt to explain why this happens. Possibly it's Source's way of getting your attention to something that was just said, or something that just happened before the outage. I can say that in my own experience, I'd made a very impactful statement defending my Twin counterpart to a friend, and all of the lights went out in a casino in Las Vegas. After several minutes when I positioned to this friend that he was a nice guy, all of the lights came back on. Source has its own way of communicating and imparting wisdom onto others. That message was not for me, but for my friend who had inserted himself, without warning, and spoke bad about my Twin. Watch thoughts and watch your words is the message from this type of sign.
- **Numbers that align to your Twin with a meaning:** Take a look at your birthdays vs. house and apartment numbers. This a telling sign. Also your Twin's birthday may align with your mother, father, niece, nephew, brother or sister's birthday. This type of numerology is not a coincidence.
- **You've established an immediate, intense connection:** The meeting was invigorating and shocking at the same time. You made eye contact that seemed to be from another time and place. You felt as though you've finally found a safe place with this person.
- **Finding coins, especially dimes:** Not much has been written about finding dimes on the Twin journey, and maybe because coins are everywhere. I can't explain the phenomena, but if

you're finding dimes in odd places, like the hood of your car, or places that seem logically irrational, chances are Source is using them to grab your attention to confirm the Twin connection during periods of separation.

Numerology 1-9

The science of numerology shows that each number has its own personality and strengths. To get a better understanding of how numbers affect us personally, it helps to know that each of these numbers carries its own unique traits and vibrations. Understanding what each number means will help you when seeing number synchronicities on repeat. Repeating of these numbers in 3's hold powerful meanings.

1. From a spiritual perspective, number 1 is the number of creation and imitating force. Seeing the numbers 111 or 1111 is the channel into the subconscious mind and considered the gateway for all manifestations to occur. Keep your thoughts positive when seeing this powerful number combination; it will manifest, be those thoughts positive or negative.
2. It's the peace and harmony number. It brings the end to separateness. It's a sign that you have planted your seeds of thoughts and now you must keep faith, even though you can't see the harvest yet. Metaphorically, it means to invest your energy into your dreams, and keep the faith that all of your work will soon pay off.
3. This number is the energy of the Trinity. It is the energy of change, or that you are" in the zone." Seeing 333 means that higher powers are watching over you, and you're receiving Divine protection, help, and guidance. In most cases it means you have the Divine helping you. Seeing 3333 means that help is coming very soon.
4. Is the number of family and home. With four, it means solid and enduring. In the spiritual significance of this number, it's the foundation for numerology meaning of "built-to-last." It is also the number of fate and protection. Seeing the number 444 is that you have nothing to fear and all is as it should be.
5. This is the number of change. Perhaps you're going through a major life change. It can also signal that a very big change is coming your way, so prepare for it now. When you see 555 this can be validation that the change you're contemplating is the best direction for you to take.

6. The meaning of 6 is the elements of earth or Gaia. It can also mean to re-evaluating what you think. Seek the truth and question your beliefs in all areas of your life. Seeing 666 can sometimes mean too much of a good thing that is really not the best for us. You may need less than you think to achieve happiness. Depending on your own religious beliefs it can represent the mark of the beast, which could translate to looking at your sins and making the necessary changes.
7. Number 7 is the seeker of truth and is also the great thinker. Release your fears, let go and find your inner strength. Seeing 777 can also mean that you are awakening to your higher-self for more wisdom and knowledge.
8. Number 8 is the number of Karma, the balance of all things materialistic. It is also the number of infinity, rebirth, and spiritual awakening. Seeing 888 is also the possibility of unlimited potential. It can also represent discipline and moderation.
9. Number 9 represents the ending of Karma, old life cycles complete, and lesson learned. Seeing 999 can be emotional and spiritual. In numerology, 9 holds the path towards mystical knowledge.

Why am I on a Twin Soul Journey?

The Twin Flame journey is to connect you to live your life's purpose so you can do what you came here to do: Step into your power and get onto your path. The Twin Flame journey is not the boy meets girl love story taken from the pages of romance novels. Each journey will be different and unique and will unfold as time passes. There is no written test to see if you have met your Twin Flame, and there is no study course in which to learn from. You just know. Twin Flames do not fit into the normal relationship models. Romanticizing the Twin Flame journey minimizes and is opposite of the Twin Flame purpose; the soul's progress and the mission you signed up for. This is not to say you can't be in a relationship with your Twin, it simply means work on *you* and see what develops. But I can assure you, if you're not willing to do the work you need to do on self, then your Twin relationship probably won't work due to the circumstances in which you were brought together; to serve a higher purpose.

- **When you're with your Twin, it's magic:** If you work together on a project, everything seems to flow. When other people step in, it goes to shit and you and your Twin become distant.
- **Your Twin Flame holds the mirror of what you fear and desire for your own inner healing:** For example, if you are high-strung, your twin flame will most likely be relaxed and easy going. If you tend to play the victim, your Twin will refuse to give you sympathy to satisfy your ego. If you are creatively challenged, your Twin will be the flourishing artist. In this way, our Twin counterpart challenges and aggravates us at the same time but, also teaches important lessons about our fears to overcoming our worst habits.
- **No matter how many times you or your Twin Flame leave, you're always magnetically attracted back to them:** (Not to be confused with abusive relationships.) Your connection has many layers. In other words, your Twin relationship is that of friend, lover, teacher, and muse all at once. One of you is more soulfully advanced than the other,

and often serves as the teacher, or confidant within the relationship.
- **Looking into the eyes of your Twin Flame can be very intense:** Because you're looking into the mirror of your own soul.
- **The feeling you have for your Twin Flame will be indescribable:** There are simply no words to describe Twin Flame love. It's soul energy that emerges when two people meet and look into the mirror of their own souls.
- **The reason for the Twin Flame connection:** To face your own unresolved issues and reach your soul's highest potential so that you can shine love and light onto the world. Physical union may or may not be part of your personal Twin journey. Every Twin couple has a different trajectory and life mission they are on. The love you share with your Twin is the highest form of love you may ever experience, however with that said, freewill choices determine a relationship. A life partner is something each person has the freewill to choose for themselves.
- **Meeting your Twin couldn't have happened at a worse time:** That is when the meeting occurs. This meeting will bring you to your knees and challenge you to the highest limits. If you're doing your own soul-level work, you'll be propelled forward. No matter how chaotic things may seem, no matter what life situations you or your Twin Flame are in, you'll be led into your journey of the soul, *by force, if needed,* so that your light can shine. That's a guarantee.

Twin Flames the Unconditional Love Story

A Twin Flame is an instant soul connection. You recognize them immediately and feel like you've known them before in another lifetime. They are part of your soul pie. You'll understand each other like no other two people ever, and be able to complete each other's sentences, have a desire to share everything with each other, and everything you thought about life will be turned upside down. Rest assured, there is nothing wrong with you when you feel this connection, and you're not going crazy when you see signs.

A Twin connection is the highest honor given to any human. It depends on how you want to look at it, but more importantly, what you do for yourself after having made the connection is what you take from the experience of meeting your mirrored soul.

The power of the Twin Flame connection is so strong that the two coming together can really make things happen and change the world. The connection between you and your Twin is that powerful, as it comes directly from Source power. This is a journey of self discovery and absolutely unconditional love for another human being without judgments-you accept them for who they are.

In the beginning of the journey you'll get along extremely well with your Twin, but the connection can become so intense that fear, doubts, questions, preconceived beliefs, and expectations of a relationship enter into the mind on both sides of the connection. The ego mind controls that, and it's the ego's of both you, and your Twin counterpart that is getting in the way of the Twin relationship that you so much desire. One of you may choose to disconnect from the relationship because of pre-conceived ego thoughts, and this is what starts the (Runner-Chaser phase.)

The pain that follows can be upsetting. The wondering *"What did I do"* ego game enters into the mind and starts fucking with you. As the (Chaser) you enter into a state of neediness.

You'll be told by friends to forget about your Twin connection and to treat it like a death. Knowing that you can never do that, but at the same time, never wanting to experience pain like that ever again. Confusion starts, and you second-guess the connection. You need validation by your Twin so you start texting and reaching out. In reality if you look at it this way, what you're chasing is yourself.

Your Twin has never left you energetically; they are actually running from themselves, especially if they have spiritual work to do.

The best thing you can do instead of chasing your Twin, is getting in the best physical condition you've ever been in, eating healthy, improving your skills, finding new and interesting hobbies, or getting out there and meeting other people casually, even if you are certain your Twin is *the one*.

Living your life and getting onto your soul's mission is the best way to open the door for your Twin to enter back into your life. Your Twin will feel the change because you're both connected energetically, and they'll feel you from a place of strength, not weakness.

I myself have gone through major changes in my life since my so-called self-induced separation period. My break from my Twin came from "expectations" I had imposed upon him, "thinking" we were in some kind of relationship after we became physical. Ego entered my brain space and he ran/ghosted again. Since our distance, I've been working out, changed careers, wrote a screenplay, and found myself inspired to write this book. You never know where your Twin journey will lead you.

The separation happens so much on the Twin journey. It's really designed by Source for each person to clean up things in their own lives and spread the message of unconditional love. Each Twin will learn and grow and become a better person because of the connection. It is from the intensity of this connection that separation occurs. The separation does not happen in every Twin Flame connection, but from my own experience and others TF's I know, it seems to be the inevitable part of the Twin journey. I talk about the Running and Chasing phase not to scare you, but to be honest. Do the work you need to do on yourself, put the Twin off to the side, and if the relationship is meant to happen, they will be moving mountains to get to you.

The bond between you and your Twin can never be severed or broken out of anger or separation or even commitments to others. The only way to break a bond, as I stated previously, if you need it severed for safety reasons, it should be done by a professional healer. This does not mean you have the right to ever stalk or pursue your Twin if they wish to go "no contact." I caution on the side of common sense, stalking anyone is not walking in the light, and you'll loose a feather in the karmic realm. Don't show up at his/her favorite place, or go looking for them. If your Twin is committed elsewhere, you need to accept the relationship he/she is currently involved in. Perhaps it is because of the lessons they need to learn from it. If you're in a "no contact" phase with your Twin, and run into them by pure Divine intervention, then the Universe is putting you together for a reason. No need to analyze the reason, and if they've chosen "no contact" that is for your Twin counterpart to sort out, not you.

I will advise this; if you take it upon yourself to create situations that is not in Divine order; recall the story of The Master and the Mature, creating situations that *magically* make you run into your Twin is not the way a Master functions, and it's not magic, it's karma, that will spank you. Remember your Twin knows everything about you, and what you're up to, as they are you. You can't hide bullshit from them, they see through it. Twin Flames are not considered "normal" relationships, so the typical dating rules do not apply to Twins. There are no games to be played, no lies to be told, and the best thing you can do to serve this relationship, is to be honest in it. This is about unconditional love.

As you get further on your journey more will be revealed to you. It took me a year to figure out what I was suppose to be doing with my life, because I'd spent a year being The Mature, analyzing and writing about signs. Save yourself a year, don't bother analyzing them. I'm here to validate you as a master in the art of manifestation. You can do that shit in your sleep, now get on with your mission.

Surrender: Choosing the Road Upward

The word *surrender* gets used a lot. Surrender does not mean leave your Twin. It means surrender to your *expectations* of what your TF relationship looks like with your Twin counterpart, or how it will be for your journey.

You're a divine infinite being who has the power to do anything in this world that you want. Your purpose is waiting for you to make the choice and when you choose it, Source is right there with you to push you upward to your calling. Never let anyone tell you you can't do something. Purpose shapes your choice. The further you move upward in making yourself a better human, the more Source is willing to work with you. When you move through the higher frequencies you evolve, as you evolve you learn, as you learn, you grow. Choosing ego takes you downward. Forget the *"why did he/she leave? I'm super awesome"* blah blah blah garbage.

The Twin mission is about energetic work. You get to choose if you spiral upward to the path you need to be on, or downward to pain and despair because your Twin is not communicating as you wish they would. The truth of who you are is not about your Twin, rather it's about you. Removing the layers of crap, and doing the inside work YOU need to do will take you where you need to be.

Surrendering is not giving up on your Twin. It is surrounding to *expectations* of having your Twin counterpart as your partner. When you love yourself, when you let go, and allow the Twin connection to be what it will be for your journey, you spiral upward and will be in alignment to your Twin connection. You already said yes to this connection. Don't get stuck and held back looking to signs for confirmation of the connection. You are connected, and you have been since the day you met your Twin Flame.

Your positive actions bring what you desire. When you're moving upward, Source will give you what you need. You don't need your Twin, you need you. If your Twin chooses to exercise their freewill and enter into a relationship with you, Awesome, you've done the work you need to do on yourself. You then get to exercise your freewill and make the decision if that is what you want; it's up to you. Either way, you need to TRUST Source, TRUST yourself, and TRUST that whatever this Twin Flame journey brings was for your highest good.

Un-F Your Vibration

The Twin Flame journey will test you like nothing before it. Keeping your vibration up is important. Some believe that the relationship with their counterpart is set in stone, so therefore leading to a false idea that no inner work needs to be done. Mantras of "set in stone" give people the illusion of *why bother with the inner work?* The inner work is the journey to your Twin. This is the reason you met. Just to be very clear, there is no Universal law that says, "*What I manifest, I get to keep. My Twin is mine forever.*" But, I see how people hold on to a belief system when they are depressed; it's easy to get caught up in messaging of energies, planetary alignments and other things that can trip you up on your journey.

There is an inner knowing that your Twin is your Divine counterpart always, however, that does not promise, or guarantee you'll be with *the one*. Some of us will reach the mountain top with our Twin and some won't, but it really depends on YOU working on your shit and un-fucking your vibration. There is no conceivable way this type of relationship model works unless both Twins are functioning on the same vibration. **Never** lower your vibration to match your Twin's, make them come up to yours. Some of the things that will help raise your vibration, and help your Twin counterpart by default, *because you are energetically connected*, is productive for you both.

1. **Find something in yourself and appreciate it** - Make a list of things you are grateful for, write down all of the things you are good at, and like about yourself. This allows you to shift the focus of lack, to appreciating yourself and all the things you have, can, and will accomplish in life. You are a beautiful powerful soul, now expand that and show yourself gratitude for being here on this planet to have the ability to be here at this great time. There is only one you, and you are unique.
2. **Eat veggies** - Believe it or not eating fresh produce raises your vibration, fast food does not raise your vibration; in fact in lowers it.

3. **Stop gossiping about others** - Gossip puts you in a very low vibration. Ask yourself, *"are the things I'm engaging in bringing me what I want?"* This holds true for social media comments, snipes, and underhanded back-smack. Don't enable friends in gossip, but politely withdraw from the conversation. What is transmitted into the Universe holds a vibration. *Hear, Speak, See no evil.*
4. **Meditate** - This helps calm you down to be in a peaceful state of mind. 10 - 15 minutes of meditation a day can change your life.
5. **Be grateful for what you have, don't focus on what you don't -** If you want more money then focus on the having of it, *not the lack of it.* If you want a partner in life then create an open space in your mind for them to come in. *Don't focus on where they are right now.*
6. **Practice acts of kindness** - Giving to someone shifts your thinking from: I don't have enough time or money. Shift that thinking to: I have more than enough to give to others. Abundance and kindness is a very high vibration.
7. **Exercise** - The more you move your body, the better you feel, the better you feel, the better experiences you will have.
8. **Get out into nature** - Nature is the best place to take your problems. Source power communes to us in nature. Connecting with Oneness is the fastest way to raise your level of vibration. The connection we share with nature has that effect on all humans, it calms us down.
9. **Salt Baths** - Warm baths are one of life's pleasures. They help melt away the day's worries and allow you to switch off your mind for awhile.
10. **Learn to say no to the things and the people that drain you** - Doing things that drain you of your energy will not make anyone around you happy. Example: If you get invited to a party and don't want to go, don't. Never feel obligated. Beliefs that we hold that we need to please others to sacrifice our own happiness is an outdated belief system. Perceptions of not attending a function that will make you "talked about" is ego. The party will go on. Ego puts us in a low vibration; stay home and watch a movie, do what you are guided to do.

11. **Smile at a stranger** - How many times have you noticed someone who looks looking defeated? A little smile goes a long long way to make someone's day just a little extra special. We've all been there. A smile costs nothing, but the rewards are good for our souls as well as the souls of those around us.
12. **Stop complaining** - Whining comes at a cost. When we complain, our brain releases stress hormones that harm our cognitive functions. This also happens when we listen to someone else complain. Give someone five minutes of ear space, then ask them if they want some cheese to go with that whine...and kindly walk away with a smile.
13. **Get off the media grid** - Whether you are trying to get more followers on Twitter, or friends on Facebook; social media has become a egocentric and pressure-sensitive environment that creates unnecessary stress in our lives. This also applies to news media outlets that create low vibrational fear mongering, that if exposed to over time, adds unneeded stress to our lives that can actually make us sick. News media is like a soap opera, you can tune in every now and then, but really...you are not missing much.
14. **Be open to others' thoughts and life experiences** - Being open-minded allows you to share in life experiences that can open you up to see things in the world differently. Not everything in the world is linear. In space-time; past, present and future exist simultaneously. Black and white are only 2-colors out of a possible 10,000,000 with many color levels of light-dark. We live in an infinite world of possibilities all with one simple word can change your life experience. Be open to others' thoughts and opinions, and watch how your life can be impacted for the better.
15. **Live a clutter free life** - Let the size of your home dictate how much stuff you keep, and not the other way around. If your closet is bursting, instead of dreaming of a bigger closet, try donating clothes and only keep the ones that fit the space you have. Rule is if you have not worn it for a season; it's time to go. Living a clutter-free life clears your mind to be more productive and creative.

16. **Loose the luxury items** - Success is not measured by the car you drive, the shoes you wear on your feet, nor the handbag you can afford to buy. Luxury stems from a feeling of lack or the "keeping up with the Jone's" mentality. Only buy it if you want it, there's no one you need to impress but you.
17. **Get over the need to compete with what others have** - Your talents, contributions and purpose in this world can never be compared to anyone else's path, nor should it. Be your own butterfly.
18. **Forgive yourself and others** - Forgiveness is compassion. Many view forgiveness as a sign of weakness. Forgiveness does not mean forget; it means to allow something or someone to go on it's merry way without attaching negative energy towards self.
19. **Practice the art of patience** - Patience requires letting go, or sitting with a quiet mind with the knowledge that the Universe gives everything in Divine timing.
20. **Keep thoughts positive and look at the signs given to you from the Universe** - Everything consists of energy and this is how synchronicity could turn into your next manifestation. Frequencies and vibrations sync together in alignment to produce these amazing experiences, and are there to guide us on our path.

Universal Laws

There were times on my Twin journey where I'd felt that I was being placed under a microscope by some Divine force. I was, the signs were there to test me to see what decisions would be made regarding my Twin. It's no coincidence that signs we are shown can be connected in someway with Universal laws.

These laws are which all people are governed by. Perhaps if we look at some of them, we could assume that we're working on some heavy duty stuff with our Twin counterpart. We are put through a series of tests in life to get us onto our path and soul missions/life purpose. Thinking about these laws made it easier for me to understand the Twin journey as a whole, not just getting into union with my counterpart. It's so much more than that.

Applying some of these laws to anything in life gives you two viewpoints to a situation that you may be working through, and insight into what your Twin could be dealing with on their side of the fence, especially during the running phase. The laws of the Universe will not only assist in your connection to your Twin, but other relationships you have in your life as well.

1. **The Universal Law of Resistance** - That which you resist you draw to you. Resistance is fear. Let go of fear when you experience it, or until you are forced to deal with it, by learning conscious detachment. *"What you resist, not only persists, but will grow in size"* - Jung
2. **The Universal Law of Harmony** - Your disharmonious actions towards all things flow out into the Universe and back upon you until your own harmony is restored. *"The harmony of natural law reveals an intelligence of such superiority that compared with it, all systematic thinking and acting of human beings is an utterly insignificant reflection"*- Einstein
3. **The Universal Law of Abundance** - You have within yourself everything required to make life as you want it. *"What you think you become. What you feel, you attract. What you imagine, you create."* - Buddha

4. **The Universal Law of Conscious Detachment** - It is your resistance that causes your suffering. Have the wisdom to accept unalterable situations as they are, without wasting physical and mental energy attempting to change what you cannot. Out of acceptance comes detachment, allowing negativity to flow through you, without resistance to affecting you personally. *"Life is changing, growth is optional. Choose wisely." -Unknown*
5. **The Law of Cause and Effect** - This law states that nothing happens by chance. Every action has a reaction or consequence. *"How you treat me is your karma. How I react is mine."* - *Unknown*
6. **The Law of Compensation** - The visible effects of our deeds are given to us in money, gifts, and blessings. "*Do not worry that your life is turning upside down. How do you know that the side you are used to is better than the one to come?*" - *Rumi*
7. **The Universal Law of Attraction** - It is how we draw things to us, to include events and people who come into our lives. Our thoughts, feelings, words, and actions produce like energy. Like attracts like, be it positive or negative. *"To attract positive things into your life, you must be positive. If you are negative you will attract negative. This is the law of attraction*" - *Unknown*
8. **The Law of Perpetual Transmutation of Energy** - All people have the power within themselves to change conditions in their lives. Higher vibrations transmute lower energies to effect the change we want to see in our lives. *"Don't downgrade your dream just to fit your reality. Upgrade your conviction to match your destiny."* - *Unknown*
9. **The Law of Relativity** - Every person will receive a series of problems for the purpose of strengthening the light within themselves. Consider each a test. Compare your problems to others' to put things in perspective. The law teaches that no matter how bad we perceive our problems, there is always someone who is in a worse position. It is all relative. *"Everything is energy. Match the frequency of the reality you want and you cannot help but get that reality. This is physics."* - *Einstein*

10. **The Law of Polarity** - Everything has an opposite. We can transform undesirable thoughts by concentrating on the polar opposite. *"Everything in the Universe has a polar opposite, in every failure, lies a success."* - Unknown
11. **The Universal Law of Rhythm** - Everything vibrates and moves to a certain rhythm. These rhythms establish seasons, cycles, and stages of development. *"Human behavior flows from three main sources: desire, emotion , and knowledge"* - Plato
12. **The Universal Law of Divine Order** - Everything is as it should be, there are no accidents, you always have opportunities to resolve karma through your thoughts, words, deeds, emotions, and actions. *"Let the world unfold without always attempting to figure it out. Let relationships just be"* - Dr. Wayne Dyer
13. **The Universal Law of Freewill** - Many major events in your life are astrologically and karma predestined. You have the freewill to mitigate the impact of any event in life. This will result in how you have lived your life up to the situation you have set-up for yourself to experience. As you obtain life awareness and develop detachment, you will be less affected from negativity by allowing it to flow out of you. You always have the freewill in how you respond to any situation. If you respond with positive emotions, compassion and integrity, you'll not have to experience a similar situation in the future. *"Life is a card game. You get the hand which you are dealt. How you choose to play that hand is your choice."* - Kris Embrey
14. **The Universal Law of Wisdom That Erases Karma**. - You can learn your lessons through love and wisdom that can mitigate your suffering. You can experience direct consequences of actions through pain, or wisdom whether in this lifetime, later in life, or a future lifetime. Past karma can be balanced in this lifetime under similar circumstances and through awareness; absolve the karma. *"Release someone from the wheel of karma by forgiving them with unconditional love, not for the hurt, but for the lesson learned and for the experience no matter how bad it may have been."* - Unknown

15. **The Universal Law of Grace** - Karma can be experienced in mercy and grace. If you give mercy and grace to others, you will receive the same in return. *"The law detects, grace alone conquers sin." - Saint Augustine*
16. **The Universal Law of Soul Evolution** - Rising above fear based emotions and expressing unconditional love will raise our vibration and move us to a state of harmony. We learn through the pain of our disharmonious acts, which can be viewed as failures. *"Sometimes you don't realize the weight of something you've been carrying until you feel the weight of it's release" - Unknown*
17. **The Universal Law of Fellowship** - When two people of a similar vibration gather for a shared purpose, their combined energy is directed to a purpose; that purpose can be doubled, tripled, and quadrupled. *"Purpose is the reason for which we live our lives, the choices we make are how we choose to exist " - Kris Embrey*
18. **The Universal Law of Reflection** - Traits you respond to in others, you recognize in yourself, both positive and negative. That which you admire in others, you see in yourself. That which you resist in others, can be found within yourself. That which you resist and react to in others, you're afraid exists in you. That which you resist, you dislike in others. *"Be a reflection of what you'd like to see in others. If you want love give love, if you want honesty, give honesty, if you want respect, give respect. You get in return what you give" - Unknown*
19. **The Universal Law of Manifestation** - Experiences create beliefs which in turn create your reality. If you are unhappy in your current reality, you must change your belief and behavior. In order for the thought to manifest into your reality, you must feel it to manifest it. *"If you can see it in your mind, then believe that it is already there." - Unknown*
20. **The Universal Law of Karma** - Until you have resolved your karma, you will continue to reincarnate. You alone decide what you need to learn and experience in this lifetime. For each life experience you seek out others to help. Those souls often are the ones you have shared histories with, but always with karmic configurations matching your needs.

Disharmonious acts must be balanced for the soul to grow.
"Forgive the person and their actions, never give in to hate, let it go, set it free, and karma will take are of what is meant to be" - Unknown

Twin Catalyst vs. True Twin Love

I had many times been told by friends that my Twin was not "the one." You'll hear everything on this journey, *"he's an asshole"* or *"he's...* (fill in the blank.)" The commonality that ties us to the Twin community seems to be the amount of synchronistic events that would be absent from the typical *organic* relationships. Whatever your specific journey will play out, it will differ from other Twin experiences. We're all on a different trajectory path that was creatively orchestrated by Source/Divine power.

Some of us will experience what is known as the catalysts, or the karmic twin that is put on our path to wake us up. This is the Twin that brings us to our knees for the really hard lessons. They are still your Twin however, they are not on your path for the romantic reason you may think. Trust in yourself, do the work you need to do, and the rest is up to you and your Twin to sort out if a relationship is in the future. If ever in doubt about this, recall the Law of Freewill. Nothing with your Twin is set in stone. Doing the work needed to be done on yourself is your best shot at the relationship you so desire with your Twin, or anyone you choose for that matter. We encounter in our lives many soul-mates, but you'll encounter only one Twin Flame. Many will disagree with this. However; I do not hold the belief of having more than one Twin connection. I believe there is only one other half to the soul, and that is why it's called Twin (meaning two) If there was more than one, it would be called something different. It's hard to fathom two or more of these types of relationships in our lives. That would be some really jacked up karma.

The one you share the most intense vibration with, meet under the strangest of circumstances, had the most synchronicities with, and the one who forces you to look inward, is your true Twin Flame.

False Twins are really nothing more than soul-mates. Not to take anything away from those experiences, because in many cases it's better than going through a Twin Flame experience due to the freewill choice in choosing those relationships. I hold the belief that Twins are fated to meet for whatever is needed for the soul to find it's true purpose or calling. This holds true for both sides of the Twin soul connection. Whether both are developed spirituality or not, both

Twin's came into this life and agreed to learn from each other, and getting into a relationship will be discovered by you and your Twin in divine timing.

The Twin Flame relationship changes your life. Each Twin will be transformed throughout their connection to each other. The relationship challenges each Twin to grow and expand into their highest potential to fulfill their life mission and purpose on the planet. Your Twin may never acknowledge you as their Divine counterpart, and it's OK, because they are your Twin no matter what anyone tells you. At some point on their journey, the other Twin will come to a realization that the time they have/had spent with you, their lives suddenly changed for the better. Whether they credit you for that change in them is irrelevant, their higher-selves know the truth.

The Dark Side of the Twin Flame Connection

The Twin Flame is the masculine and feminine side within two people. So why all the drama? You and your Twin are here to purge, get on the path of doing your life's mission and if you are to be together and that is how the soul contract was written, you will. No time line, or tarot reader can tell you when; it's called Divine timing, only God and your spirit team will know the answer. You and your Twin will not only experience things being purged, but you can experience the more jacked-up elements of polarity. The light and dark shadows sides of self, and it's your Twin holding a bright flashlight on those shadows. You can't have dark without light. We experience that in our everyday lives when we wake-up in the morning and go to bed at night.

Connecting with your Twin Flame in this lifetime, you signed-up to learn, embrace and clear those elements of your own shadows, because everybody has a shadow and everybody has repressed crap that lives inside of us. Twin Flame connections give you the opportunity to clear out those shadows, and it can be beyond uncomfortable, because you can experience the more extreme elements through your Twin; not just in the personality of the person you are connecting with, but the blood lines of past generations-characteristics from family history will come up over and over on your journey; issues of abandonment, narcissism, wrongful doings, past hurts, the list goes on and on. Your clearing out each other's garbage and bloodlines.

When the soul has chosen to experience different elements of the human experience, the soul might choose to experience the light and love, or the darkest depths of hell. I must have chosen to see hell, because I've gone thru a year of "the dark night of the soul" and purge more of the darker elements of my Twin. My Twin carries narcissist tendencies. These would be considered ancestral issues, locked into his DNA, and because I feel my Twin, I take on the darker elements of his crap and purge it for him, without him knowing, as he has no knowledge of what a Twin Flame is or does.

We all have elements of that dark that lay within us, but never will the experience of those dark elements be more extreme than with the highest soul connection-your Twin Flame. It's because the intensity between Twins goes back to a time before birth. It may be that your soul chose for you to experience crazy separation, and extreme high and lows. But also it can play out, that one of you can be experiencing very much the light coming from the heart, while the other can be experiencing the darker elements, from past lives or ancestry crap. It can change according to how the soul contract was set up before you were born. But it can also change according to outside interference from others. And this gets crazy. When you come into an intense soul connection like a Twin Flame, it can trigger a massive amount of negativity between the two of you, and all the people immediately around you (this would include your parents, siblings, friends, even co-workers). Your connection to your Twin can trigger baggage/garbage in other people that can trigger stuff in them; their own judgments of you, feelings of what love is, or should be, what relationships are, and how *they believe need to be defined*, their own personal hang ups, but mostly, a ton of jealousy, a lot of hostility, guilt, and all kinds of "shit" that is not you or your Twin's stuff. It is this outside interference that can really f-up your connection to your Twin, and it sucks.

These very same people can interfere with your union, either directly by voicing it or indirectly by manipulation and control; even going as far as to bring the union down. How can something as strong as Twin Flame love ever be brought down? The opposite of love is hate, and outside influences can have a negative effect on the union and on the Twins themselves. This negativity can be instrumental in bringing down your Twin Flame union. It was tried on me twice by two different people, the last person sent my Twin running. It is very real and don't think it can't happen; it does, but karma sucks, and no need to pray for karma on someone who knowingly or unknowingly did wrong by you, Source may have orchestrated this for a Divine reason-a lesson for you to learn from.

Everything is energy and the energy of love is very strong in Twins, but that love can also experience interference from negative and dark energies. These would be considered entities. Twins can actually be targeted. I have experienced a direct target from a "former friend" to take down my union with my Twin; he wasn't successful. Why would Twins be targeted? Why would their be vested interest in taking down a powerful loving connection? Because it is a very powerful union. There is vested interest in taking down a powerful loving connection if you're not of the love and light. The dark side is very real.

Past, present and future exist at the same time. When you've had a past connection with someone, it is a very powerful connection, much more powerful than meeting someone organically and having a *normal* attraction to them. The Twin Flame connections are designed that way. Our souls decided to be born at this time, and experience the way it is to be now in order to learn and grow. The idea here is to cleanse out any mental, emotional issues, and family histories from the template. More Twins seem to fall into this category. When you have a high level soul connection, all this garbage comes into play and you have to deal with it. You and your Twin counterpart are both very much loved by Source power, and Source wants you both to be happy in life. You are very powerful beings; you would not have been chosen to connect together in this lifetime, if you were not.

As you go further along on this journey, you'll meet people who will serve as your guide as you expand your knowledge, and as you expand that knowledge, you'll become more elevated spirituality and learning life lessons as you evolve and grow then you'll be guided to new teachers that will take you to the next phase of learning. Not everyone graduates at the same time, but we all do. Age has no factor in soul development. We learn and grow as we apply life lessons, and move to the next grade. We keep evolving and growing. It is a beautiful and rewarding process.

It takes faith to be on this journey. Never give up on yourself and have faith in your Divine counterpart by surrendering your fear-based ego mind, and *allow the relationship to happen.*

Blessings to you all. I hope this information helps you on your Twin journey. I want nothing but the very best for you now, and always.

About the Author

Imagine yourself completing your very first romance fiction novel and secure a publisher. Sounds good so far. But let's say there's a possibility you will meet the antagonist from your fiction story in real life. Would you change the antagonist storyline?

Hollywood has done countless movies on the subject of manifestation. The Matrix is one example, but could you see yourself living within a real life matrix? It happened just after my first book was released in March 2016 by Archway Publishing. Life as a writer took an interesting turn when fictional characters started to show up on my path.

What I'd believed and thought about the spiritual world, would be challenged the day I'd met Mark Grant, and hearing the name Lex Lenord being paged over a P.A. system. Knowing this was more than a mere coincidence, as these were two fictional names used in my romance novel.

One afternoon, and the same week my first book was published, I was reviewing a profile from a dating site I'd joined. The man who I'll call "Ray," messaged me while I'd looked up at the sky, being memorized by a rainbow on a clear day. Replying back to Ray's message, he seemed interested in meeting for coffee, making a plan to meet later in the week.

That following Monday, sitting at work, Ray sent a message to see if we could meet-up for a drink after work. On that same day, I'd gotten my e-book stubs in the mail from Archway, and my first book was now officially published. Putting a few in my purse, heading out the door, I set out to go meet Ray.
At the bar we ordered drinks and proceeded to have a great conversation. Talking with him, it felt like I'd known him a really long time, which was kind of unusual for me to hit it off with someone that fast. We paused and started looking into each others eyes and it got intense, "I really like you," he said, with a smile, wanting to know what I was thinking. Being to shy to answer back, only offering him a smile in his direction, he smiled back. What I

really wanted to say was, "Where have you been my entire life?" but the words didn't come out. Our conversation would continue to flow the entire evening, as he asked questions of me being a writer. Reaching into my handbag, I pulled out one of the book stubs I'd gotten earlier that day, handing one to him, stating that I never expected him to ever read my romance novel. We continued to talk for a few more hours, then decided to end the night when he walked me to my car.

A few days passed after our date, and the friend who suggested I join the dating site, was in town for work. The hardbound version of my book had just delivered to my door. Pulling the books from the box, my friend had arrived at my house. I didn't give my friend time to settle in, excitement took over my mouth telling him about Ray, babbling on how I met this great guy, thanking my friend for the suggestion to join the dating site. Grabbing my phone to show a photo that Ray and I, had taken at the bar. My friend was standing over my books sitting on the table, as he started to get a very odd facial expression while doing a double take of the books sitting on my table. My friend picked-up my book said, "are you kidding me? Look at this," taking my phone to enlarge the photo, laid it next to my book; astounding to find that we were looking at the same person. "You didn't show Ray this did you?" My friend demanded, positioning that I did give Ray a book stub, but hadn't noticed the similarity to the illustrated book cover. "You manifested this guy." My friend said, laughing shaking his head at me, as he walked away into the other room. I do admit, it was shocking to see the similarity of the cover art illustrated by a former co-worker several months before I met Ray, the resemblance was a dead-ringer.

Over the course of the next year I became friends with Ray. His personality traits were being slowly revealed to me, and I would come to learn that he and the antagonist Sebastian, were one in the same. In these months of developing a friendship with Ray, synchronicity would connect him to my fiction story published with Archway. Sebastian had a specific story line that was to be completed in a three-part series. Now what do I do?

Manifestation at the basic core principal "like attracts like" which in philosophy is used to sum up the idea that by focusing on thoughts, a person brings positive or negative experiences into their life. I'd spent around nineteen-hours a day, seven days a week, over the course of three-months writing my book. I guess manifestation of my antagonist was an inevitability waiting to happen. To say I was attached to my writing would be an understatement. I'd spent more time developing Sebastian, than other characters in the book. Sebastian came to life from cover to cover literally, and confirmed to me, a classic case of manifestation.

Synchronicities are the simultaneous occurrence of events that appear significantly related but have no discernible causal connection. Many experiences perceived as coincidence are due not merely to chance, but instead potentially reflected by the manifestation of coincident events or circumstances. Manifesting is the intention to create something. Focusing with great detail on my antagonist Sebastian, seems I'd brought into my life experience his doppelganger, Ray.

Can manifestation of a fiction story really happen? Yes, it can. Perhaps The Matrix is more than just the work of science fiction. When you're in the "zone" focused and developing characters, what is written can come to pass. It happened to me. Perhaps the best advice I can give any new romance author…write your own love story of how you'd want to see it play out, especially if your single, you might just meet the love of your life.

Kris Embrey is the author of Tell Me You Want Me, and Till the Other Side of Time. Archway Publishing.

Website: https://www.tellmeyouwantme.com/
Facebook Page: tell me you want me

Made in the USA
Monee, IL
22 June 2022